No Sacrifice Too Great

Book 7 of the Junior Jaffray Collection of Missionary Stories

Written by Barbara Hibschman

Illustrated by Elynne Chudnovsky
Cover Design by Step One Design
Portrait by Karl Foster
Based on *No Sacrifice Too Great* by Ruth Presswood Hutchins

CHRISTIAN PUBLICATIONS / Camp Hill, Pennsylvania

The mark of vibrant faith

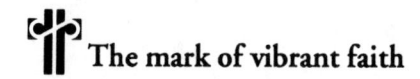

Christian Publications
Publishing House of The Christian
and Missionary Alliance
3825 Hartzdale Drive, Camp Hill, PA 17011

© 1993 by Christian Publications
All rights reserved
ISBN: 0-87509-515-1
Printed in the United States of America

93 94 95 96 97 5 4 3 2 1

Unless otherwise indicated, Scripture taken from the HOLY BIBLE: NEW INTERNATIONAL VERSION. Copyright © 1973, 1978, 1984 by the International Bible Society. Used by permission of Zondervan Bible Publishers.

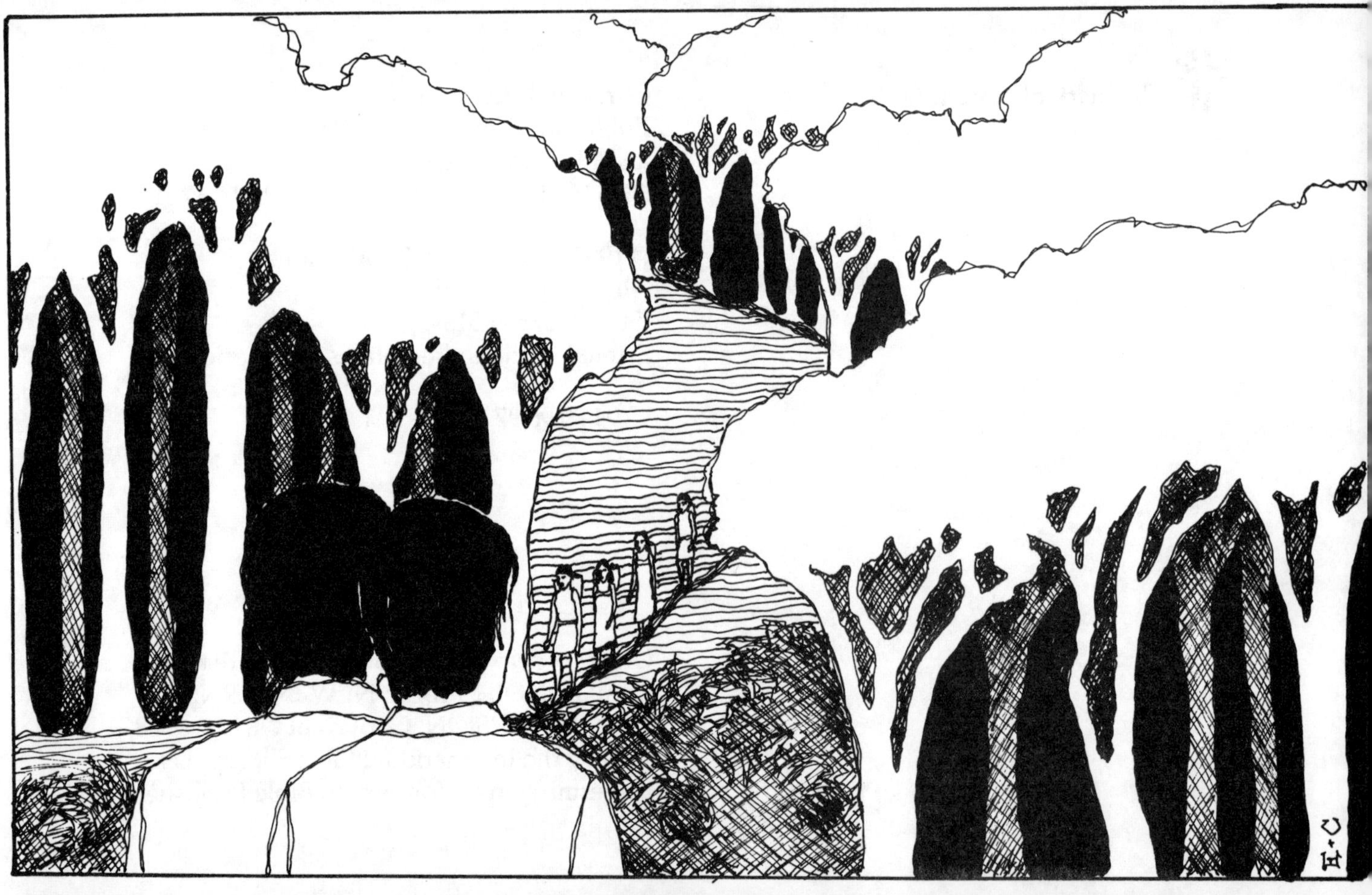

Chapter 1

Easter with the Dyaks

Ernie Presswood and John Willfinger were missionaries. They lived in Borneo, an island far away from where you live. One Easter Sunday morning, Ernie and John were awakened by a strange noise.

The noise sounded far away. They looked out the window, but they couldn't see a thing because it was still dark.

"That noise sounds like people crying," said Ernie.

John put his ear closer to the window. "Let's go outside so we can hear better," he suggested.

The two men stepped out into the warm night and stood in the Mission yard.

"Why, that's not crying," exclaimed Ernie. "That's singing!"

"You're right," agreed John. "Those Dyaks must have gotten up awfully early to be here already."

"Tramp, tramp, tramp" sounded all the bare feet as they kept beat with the music. Hundreds of brown-skinned Dyaks were marching in a long line down the mountain path through the jungle. And while they walked, they sang songs about Jesus.

Soon John could see the first ones in the line.

"Look, Ernie," he said, "they are carrying something on their backs. What is it?"

"It's their Easter offerings," replied Ernie who had already celebrated quite a few Easters with the Dyaks. "They have no money, but since they harvested their rice crops, they are bringing rice as an offering to the Lord. We can sell the rice and use the money to build churches. Even though the Dyaks are poor, they've learned to give God part of what they have."

On and on the Dyaks came down the mountain. Soon the yard was filled with smiling faces. These Dyaks loved the Lord Jesus Christ and many of them had walked for six or eight days just so they could bring their offerings to the church and celebrate Easter with Ernie and John.

Ernie was the first missionary to tell the Dyaks how they could have eternal life. When he first arrived in Borneo no one knew anything about God and His love. He taught them John 3:16. Maybe you know that verse already: "For God so loved the world that he gave his one and only Son, that whoever believes in him shall not perish but have eternal life."

The Dyaks had listened carefully when Ernie told them how God sent His Son to die on a cross for their sins. They were tired of their old ways. They lived in fear. They didn't get along with their neighbors. They fought and even killed each other. They lied and stole from each other.

When Ernie told them that Jesus could give them peace in their heart, they were ready to listen. And the more they listened, the more they wanted to live God's way. Hundreds and hundreds of Dyaks asked Jesus to forgive their sins and come into their hearts.

No wonder these Dyaks were singing and smiling on Easter Sunday. They had a new life, filled with joy and peace.

It was a very happy Easter for the Dyaks and for the missionaries who had brought them the good news.

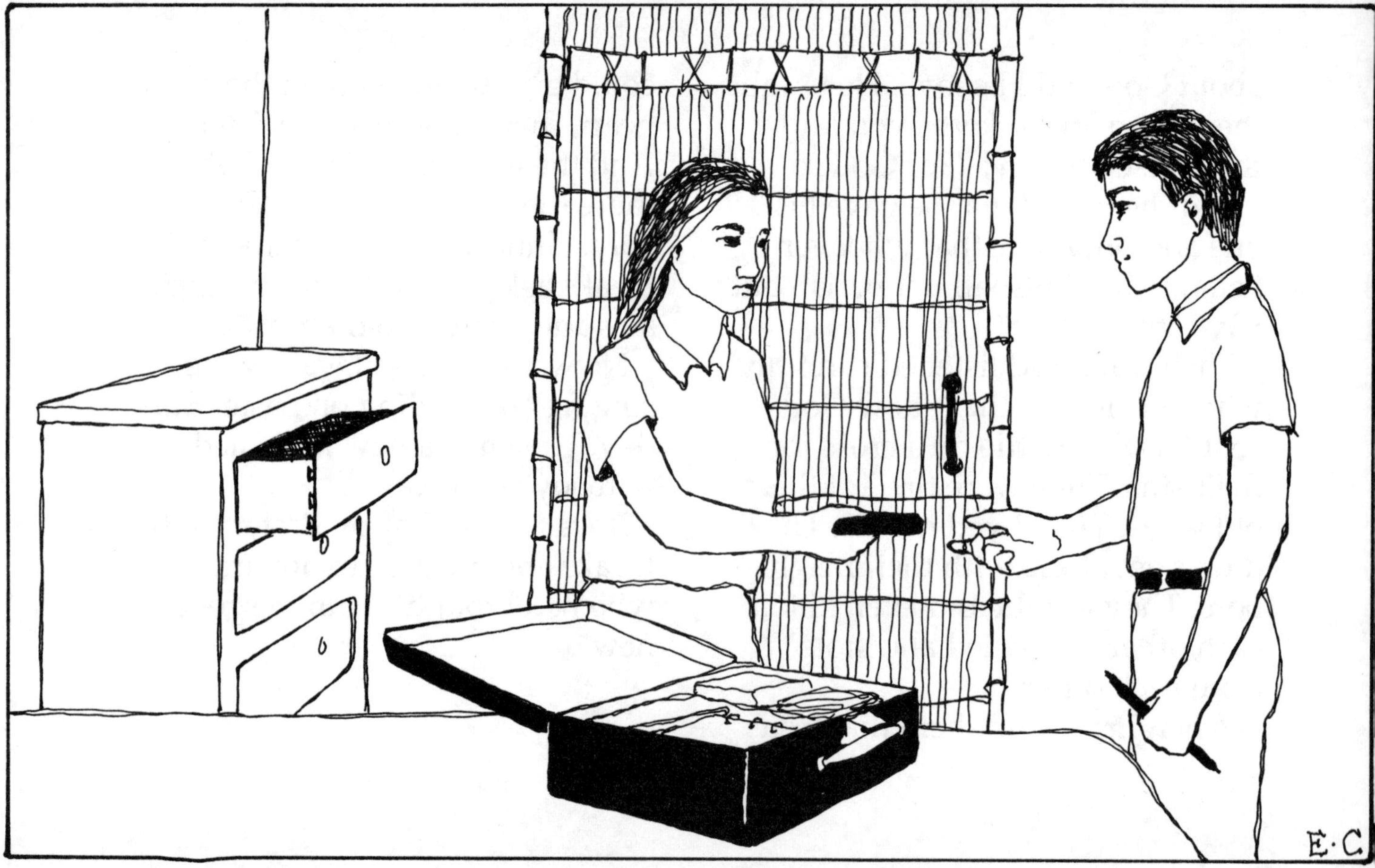
E·C.

Chapter 2

The Secret Message

Have you ever sent someone a secret message? One time, Ernie Presswood sent his wife, Ruth, a secret message in a pen!

Ernie and Ruth had just returned to their island home when they heard some news that changed the rest of their lives. It was not good news. In fact, it was bad news. A big war had just begun. Japanese soldiers were landing on the shores of their island.

Ernie and Ruth heard that the Japanese soldiers were close to where they lived. So they went to a place up in the mountains called Benteng Tinggi. It was cool up there and the view was beautiful. Eight other missionaries were there, too. *How many days will it be until the Japanese find us*, they all wondered.

A few days later the Japanese soldiers arrived at Benteng Tinggi.

"They're here," Ernie told Ruth as he burst into the bedroom. "I have only five minutes to get ready."

"Get ready for what?" asked Ruth.

"They're taking all of the men away for questioning," Ernie explained.

Ernie got his little black suitcase and started taking things out of the dresser. Ruth helped him pack some clothes, a toothbrush, a shaving kit and a notebook.

Ruth handed Ernie her Bible. It was smaller than his and easier to carry. Then she gave him her special pen. It was special because it had ink in one end and a pencil in the other.

The five minutes passed by too quickly. Ernie had to go. He and Ruth prayed a short prayer together and gave each other a hug.

Saying "goodbye" to someone you love is a hard thing to do, especially if you don't know when you will be able to see them again. It was very hard for Ernie and Ruth to leave each other. Ruth had no idea if the soldiers would hurt Ernie. *I wonder if I'll ever see him again*, she asked herself.

As Ruth watched the truck drive down the road to the highway, she prayed, "Dear God, please keep

Ernie safe and help me to be strong."

Ruth prayed for Ernie many times a day and read God's Word to find Bible verses that would help her be strong. She found one in Philippians 4:13. It said, "I can do everything through him [that means God] who gives me strength." That verse was God's special message to Ruth when she felt like she couldn't wait anymore.

Seven months went by—that's over 200 days! Ruth had not heard anything from Ernie. She didn't know where he was or if he was sick or hurt.

Then, one day a man on a bicycle arrived at Benteng Tinggi. Ruth opened the door.

"It's from Mr. Presswood," the man said as he handed her the pencil. Before Ruth could talk to him, the man rode away.

Ruth stared at the pencil. It was her own special pencil—the one that had a pencil at one end and a pen with ink on the other end. *Something must have happened to Ernie*, she thought, *Why else would he have sent this to me?*

Ruth made a few marks on a piece of paper. The pencil worked. Then she tried to write with the pen. It didn't work. She unscrewed the pen. *No wonder it doesn't work,* Ruth thought to herself. *It doesn't have any ink in it!* Instead of ink, there was a little piece of paper rolled up like a scroll inside the pen.

It was a note from Ernie—a secret message!

"He's alive!" Ruth gasped. She was so excited she ran and told the other missionaries. She had to be very careful that the Japanese guards didn't find out because no one was supposed to visit the missionaries nor were they to talk to anybody else.

Ruth carefully unrolled the note from Ernie.

"I'm all right," it said. "Rice, sometimes fruit and vegetables to eat. Men will be moved. . . . I love you. Ernie."

Ruth was so happy and thankful. "Thank you, Lord, for getting Ernie's secret message to me," she prayed. "Thank you that he is alive. Thank you for the strength you give us each day."

CHAPTER 3

My Friend Jackie

Sometimes things happen to us that are hard to understand. Maybe your best friend moved away and you feel lonely. Or maybe your Mommy and Daddy got a divorce.

The Bible says that Jesus understands how we feel and He has the power to help us.

Ruth Presswood felt very lonely at Benteng Tinggi. Ernie had been taken away by the Japanese soldiers and she didn't know when she would see him again.

It helped to have other missionaries at Benteng Tinggi. At least they could talk and pray with each other. But there were other friends at Benteng Tinggi, too—Trippi and Jackie—dogs that belonged to Dr. Jaffray.

Trippi was the oldest and acted like it. (You may have already read about him in Book One of this series, *Let My People Go*.) Sometimes when Trippi was spoken to, he just grunted back. At other times he would stick his nose in

13

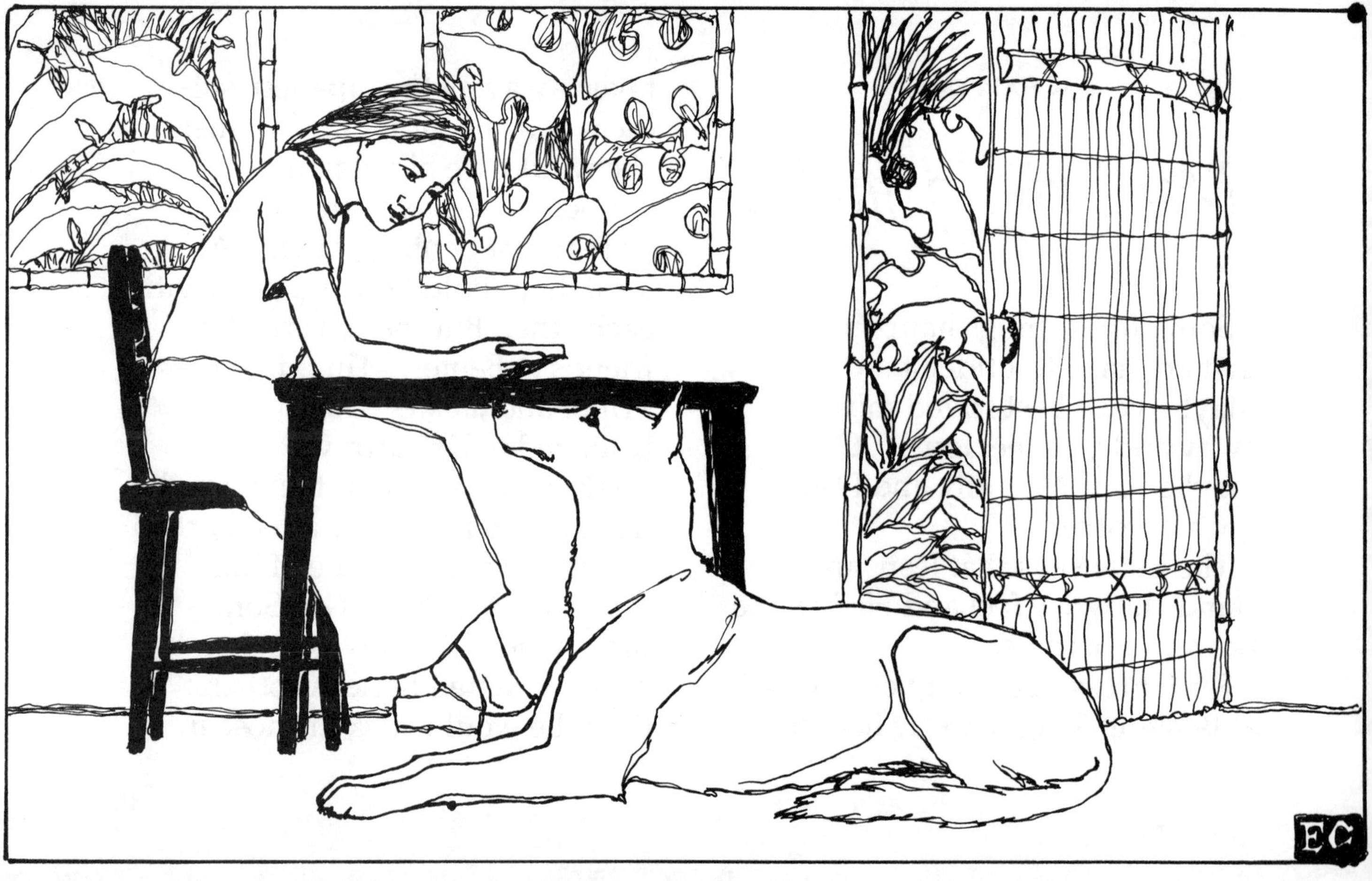

the air and walk right on by. Ruth enjoyed watching him strut through the house with his long body and short legs.

Jackie was taller than Trippi and looked like a hunting dog with short brown hair. Whenever someone spoke to him, he came immediately, his tail wagging. He liked to sit near people and look up at them with big, friendly, understanding eyes.

After Ernie Presswood was taken away by the soldiers, Jackie seemed to understand that Ruth felt lonely. Every morning he would push open the door to Ruth's room, walk in, and lay down in a patch of sunlight underneath her desk, close to her feet.

Every night Ruth and the other missionaries met to read the Bible and pray together. Trippi and Jackie were always there, too. Jackie always found a place near Ruth's feet. Sometimes he would rub himself against her leg or push his nose underneath her hand so she would pet him.

Of course, you know dogs can't talk. But Ruth felt like he was telling her, "Hello, I'm your friend. I'll be here when you're lonely."

Ruth couldn't change anything

about the war. She couldn't do anything about the Japanese soldiers taking Ernie away.

But God had said in His Word: "Never will I leave you" (Hebrews 13:5).

Ruth was thankful for that promise. She asked God to remind Ernie of that same promise, too, when he was lonely.

Chapter 4

The Forest Fire

It was the dry season at Benteng Tinggi. Borneo did not have four seasons like we do in the United States and Canada—spring, summer, fall and winter. In Borneo they had just two seasons—rainy and dry.

The mountains and the valleys that once looked liked green velvet at Benteng Tinggi had now turned brown. It was the dry season and there had been no rain for a long time.

When grass and leaves turn brown and dry, it is easy for fires to start. That is exactly what happened.

One day Ruth Presswood was sitting at her desk when she smelled smoke. She opened the door. The yard was on fire. The dry grass and trees around the house were burning.

"Come quick! We're in trouble," yelled Ruth. Soon all the missionaries had gathered near the house. "Let's fill up the buckets and pour water on the ground in

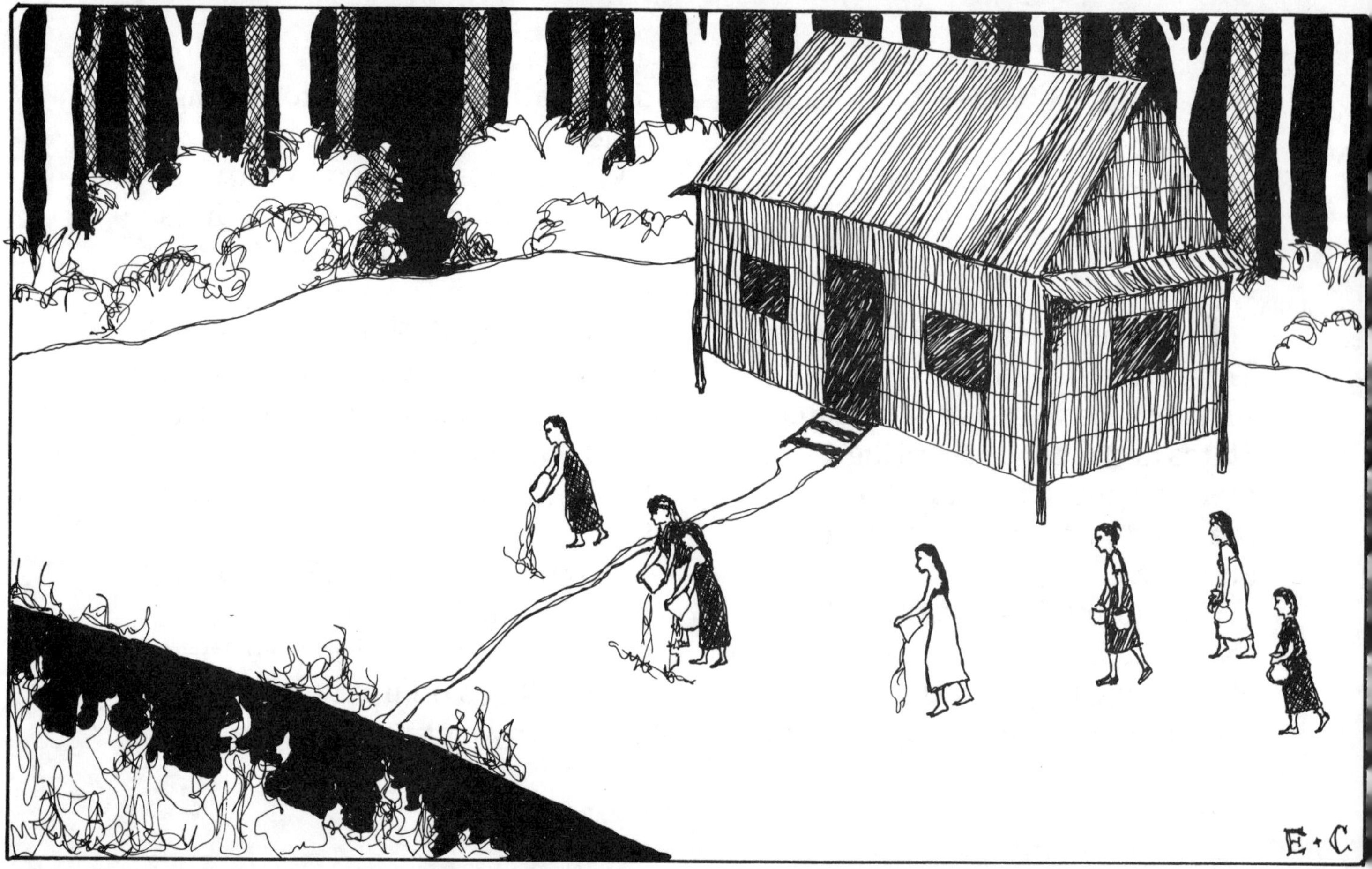
E·C

front of the houses. Maybe that will stop the fire!" someone suggested.

The missionaries filled up their buckets and poured water all around the houses. But they soon realized that a few buckets of water couldn't stop a forest fire.

"Oh God," they prayed, "please stop the fire."

Just as the hot flames reached one of the houses, a very strange thing happened. God did something special—He made the wind change direction. Instead of blowing the fire toward the house, the wind blew the flames away from the house.

It was a miracle! God had answered their prayer!

That night, the missionaries gathered for Bible reading and prayer. They all knew God had done something very special for them that day.

"Thank you, God," they prayed, "for sparing our house and maybe even our lives, too!"

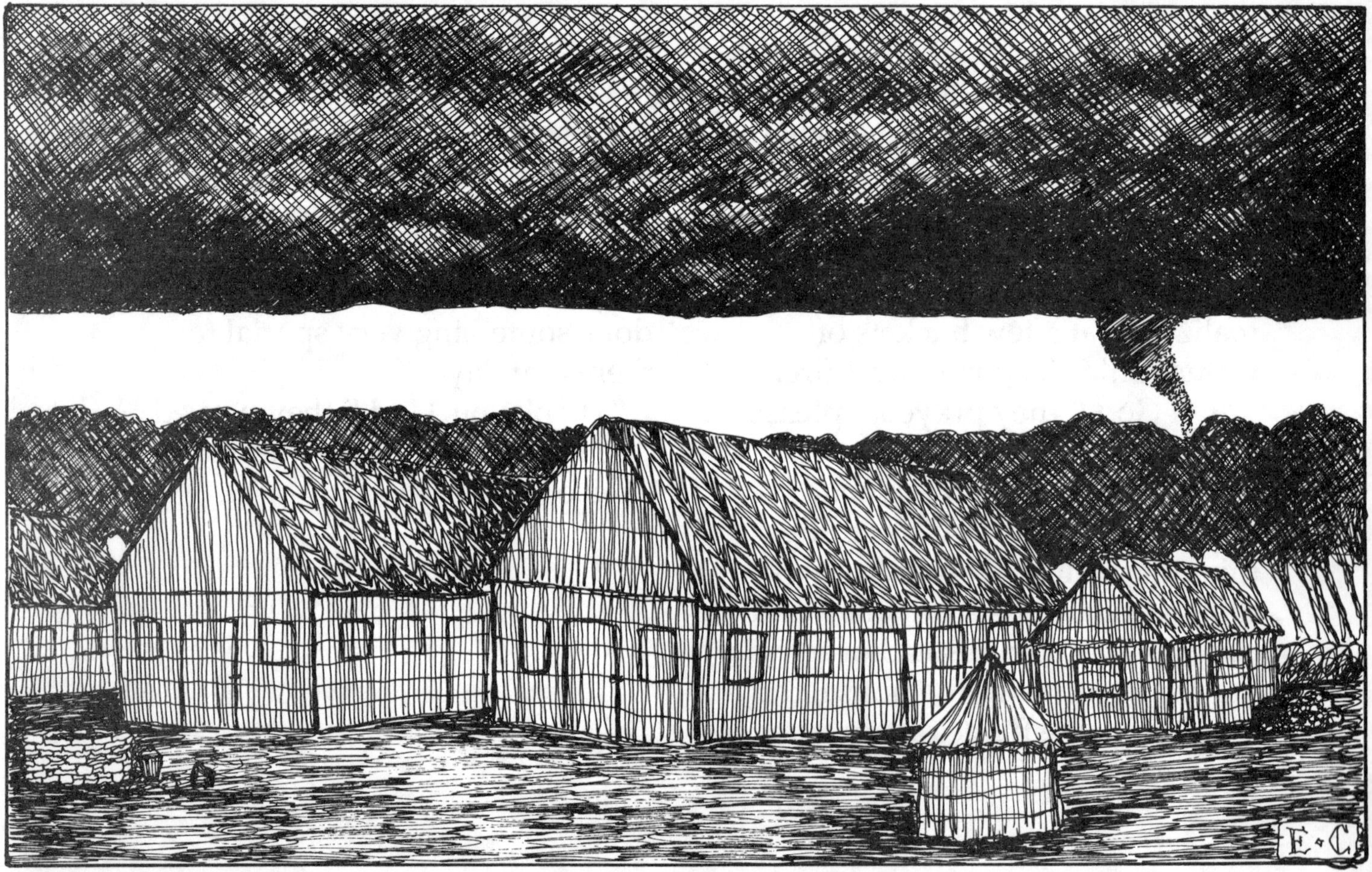
E·C

Chapter 5

A Safe Place to Hide

Have you ever been afraid and looked for a safe place to hide? This story is about how God provided a safe place to hide in a scary place—a prison camp called Kampili.

When Ruth arrived at Kampili, she noticed there were tall barbed-wire fences around rows of long bamboo buildings. Each building had 100 bunk beds where the women prisoners would sleep. Ruth chose a top bunk.

The women prisoners worked very hard. They had to carry water in buckets from a well, dig ditches, collect bundles of wood and carry big sacks of rice on their backs.

One day, Ruth was ordered to cook rice for 100 people. But there was just one problem—there was no wood to make a fire. Ruth knew that she could be punished if she didn't get the rice cooked.

Ruth looked everywhere for wood. She managed to find a few

little, dry twigs. But it takes a lot of wood to build a fire to cook that much rice.

While Ruth looked for wood she noticed the sky getting dark even though it was morning. Big, black odd-looking clouds were heading toward Kampili.

"A tornado is coming," the Japanese commander shouted. "Take shelter!"

The women started to run, looking for a safe place to hide from the tornado. Ruth raced back to her building. The rain was coming down fast and hard. Doors were slamming in the wind. Ruth helped to close the windows and doors, then she huddled with some other women in one corner of the building.

The wind whistled and roared. Some of the women screamed. Others started to cry. Ruth prayed quietly, asking the Lord to keep them safe. She knew a bamboo building was not a safe place to be in a tornado, but it was a safe place if God was there with them.

"You are my hiding place, you will protect me from trouble," Ruth said as she remembered the memory verse she had learned in Sunday School.

God is more powerful than the storm, Ruth thought to herself. *He knows all about the tornado and He knows all about me.*

After the storm was over, Ruth rushed outside. She wanted to see what damage had been done. The kitchen was now nothing but a pile of bamboo sticks. The shed where the rice was kept was gone, too. But every building that had people in it was still standing. No one had been hurt.

When the sun broke through the clouds later that day two beautiful rainbows were shining over Kampili Camp. Ruth looked up in the sky and thanked God for protecting everyone from the tornado.

He had provided a safe place to hide.

And now Ruth's job of finding enough wood to make a fire to cook rice was not a problem anymore. There were bamboo sticks everywhere!

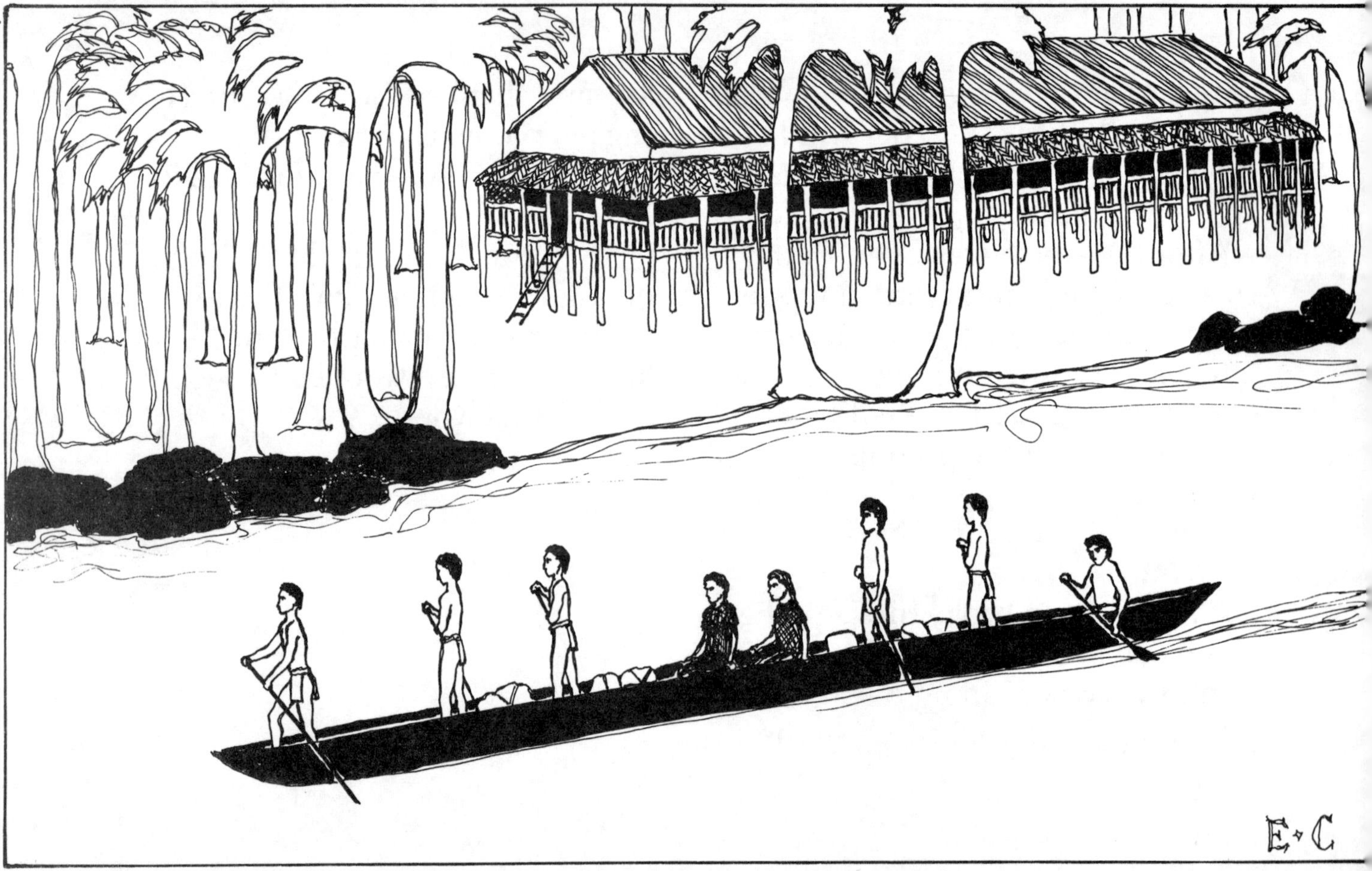

Chapter 6

The Dangerous Canoe Trip

The war was over! It had been three and one-half years since Ernie and Ruth had seen each other.

Japanese soldiers took Ruth from Kampili Camp to a house in a nearby city. A few days later Ernie arrived at the same house. How glad they were to see each other! How thankful they were to be alive!

When Ruth and Ernie got a little stronger and it was safe to travel, can you guess where Ernie wanted to go? Yes, he wanted to go back and see the Dyaks, the same ones he had spent that happy Easter with.

But that was a long and dangerous journey through the jungles of Borneo. There were no roads. The only road was the river. And they didn't travel by car—they went in a very long dugout canoe.

Day after day the canoe swayed from side to side as the hired men propelled it up the river. When the water was deep they paddled. When the water was shallow, they used long poles and pushed the canoe.

Big rocks and water falls made the trip very dangerous. The river was also full of crocodiles, snakes and leeches. The canoe could easily get stuck on a rock or tip over in the raging rapids. It took four days just to get through the rapids.

Finally, as Ernie and Ruth got closer to the Mission house, they could hear the Dyaks yelling: "The missionaries are coming! The missionaries are coming!" The Dyaks lined up on the banks of the river, greeting the missionaries with big smiles.

Ruth felt very strange. She had not seen the Dyaks before. They stared at her. She tried not to stare back. There were flies and dirt everywhere.

The Dyak women cooked rice in big iron kettles and roasted meat over an open fire. Can you guess what they used for dishes? Banana leaves! At least no one had to wash dishes! And, instead of using forks and spoons, they just used their fingers.

Bath time was different, too.

There were no bath tubs or showers. Ruth took her bath in the river like the Dyaks. Not only did the water feel like ice, but hundreds of tiny fish nipped at her all over.

The Dyaks didn't look like Ernie and Ruth. Their skin was a different color and their way of doing things was different, too. But their hearts were the same.

Ernie and Ruth were there on the island of Borneo because Jesus said, "Go into all the world the preach the good news...."

God loved the Dyaks so much that He gave His Son to die for the Dyaks. Ernie and Ruth Presswood loved the Dyaks, too.

**THE JUNIOR JAFFRAY
COLLECTION OF MISSIONARY STORIES**
For additional copies of *No Sacrifice Too Great* or information about other titles in the **Junior Jaffray Collection of Missionary Stories**, contact your local Christian bookstore or call Christian Publications toll-free at 1-800-233-4443.

*Titles coincide with the adult biography series, **The Jaffray Collection of Missionary Portraits**.